Super Sammy
Angelic Scottie

Life Story of a Terrier's Terror to Triumph

Joy Smith Walsh

Super Sammy
Angelic Scottie
Life Story of a Terrier's Terror to Triumph
Joy Smith Walsh

Published July 2024
Little Creek Books
Imprint of Jan-Carol Publishing, Inc.
All rights reserved
Copyright © 2024 Joy Smith Walsh
Photographs and Artwork: Contributed
Graphic Design: Tara Sizemore

This book may not be reproduced in whole or part, in any manner whatsoever without written permission, with the exception of brief quotations within book reviews or articles.

ISBN: 978-1-962561-31-0

Jan-Carol Publishing, Inc.
PO Box 701
Johnson City, TN 37605
publisher@jancarolpublishing.com
www.jancarolpublishing.com

Dedicated to:
Andy
Bea
Randolph "Randy" Scott
Micky
Shelby Dean
Bobby Magee
Logan
Peyton Tyler
Lucy Belle
Blue
Marty
Bonnie
Monty (Scottie Grand Pup)
These are Scotts I've been privileged to have enrich my life over the years.
We've had Cricket for six years now.

Also Dedicated to:
The Tennessee Scottie Rescue, Ginger and Jim McAfee,
and to more than 500 faithful followers of Sammy and his many life lessons.

Sammy Walsh

Sammy's History

Once in a lifetime, a special pet comes into your life. Sammy was that one! I picked up this bedraggled Scottish terrier from Jim McAfee Scottie Rescue. Sammy's tongue was hanging out of his mouth, his ears were gnarled looking, and he had terrible skin conditions from being on the streets. Sammy surveyed his new surroundings and fellow Scotties. This little worn-out dog had to learn trust, love, and be comfortable knowing his food and water was always available.

If anything could be done for him to help hold his tongue in, we were willing to try. It was humbling leaving the vet's office. Even the technicians were in tears after assessing Sammy's condition. They stopped counting breaks and fractures. His ears would never stand most likely from frostbite he received as a pup, or some trauma. Four implants were not possible due to the violence of his extractions. The burn scars would eventually be covered with hair.

So, our journey with an "ethereal" little canine began, and his attributes and antics grew to the tune of more than 500 followers on social media. Sammy was sent to be shared and inspire so very many people, including all his aunts and uncles. Boy, did we all get reminded of what life is supposed to be about through the eyes of two chestnut brown eyes belonging to this little Scottie. We were reminded of forgiveness. Sammy was the epitome of forgiveness!

We were reminded that there is indeed "unconditional love," reminded that we should not "judge a book by its cover," and reminded that hopelessness can be loved back into this little canine spirit as well as people. Sammy exuded humbleness at all times, and to watch his very spirit, essence, and physical health grow was awe-inspiring. We received so much love and support from his fanbase. We all continued to marvel at Sammy's natural magnetic personality and the fact that not only did he exude an aura during the day, but also, he literally *glowed* in the dark. That's ethereal!

His story and lessons touched so many hearts across the world. We had Sammy for 500 days before he took his wings back to heaven.

The shock and grief across the world at Sammy's loss was palliative. Condolences, flowers, and tributes poured into our home — so many permanent memorials that are still honoring him.

This little Scottie gave out so many "heart patches" that remain with so many special people I consider friends, and although we may never meet in person, we were all joined by this little angel.

We all need reminders of worth, presence, and unconditional love.

Five Lessons in Life

1: Forgiveness

I thank you for being mean to me!
I would have never met my new parents.
I would not have the unconditional love and patience that I experienced.

2: Trust

Wounded and crusty heart, learning to be open.

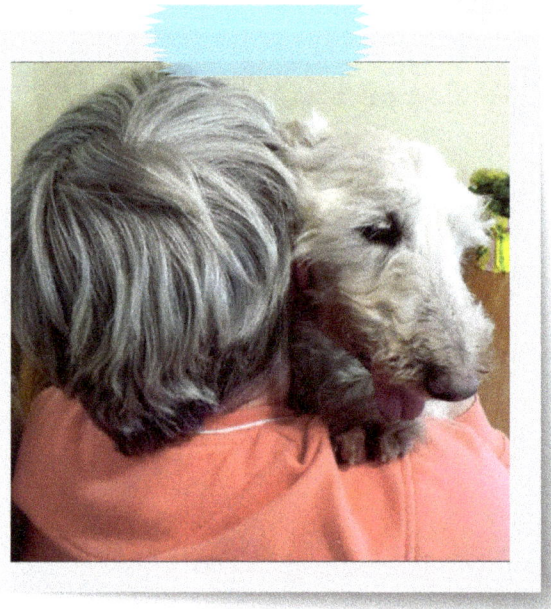

Under the scabs beats a loving heart.

Trace my stripes; they became trails of faith.

3: Strength in Adversity

Spirit starvation

Spiritual hunger

It takes strength to endure — to just "be."

4: Love Unconditionally

It doesn't matter now...I will give of my love, no matter what.

Dip into the well of love; it is soul-refreshing!

I give because I can, and I choose to.

To love and be loved is feeling the sun from both sides.

5: Mission Fulfillment

Do something with your love.

What is your love's purpose?

Tap your heart and let the flow happen (it might be good).

Tap a keg, and you know what to expect.
But you never really know what you are getting until you get it.

Sometimes, you don't know
your heart until you share it!

Sometimes, we think we are one thing, when we are really another.
Maybe, just maybe, you are not as bad as you thought.

Can you see Sammy? He's everywhere. Can you see Sammy's traits in your life?

Battle Scars

From a war that was never his to fight

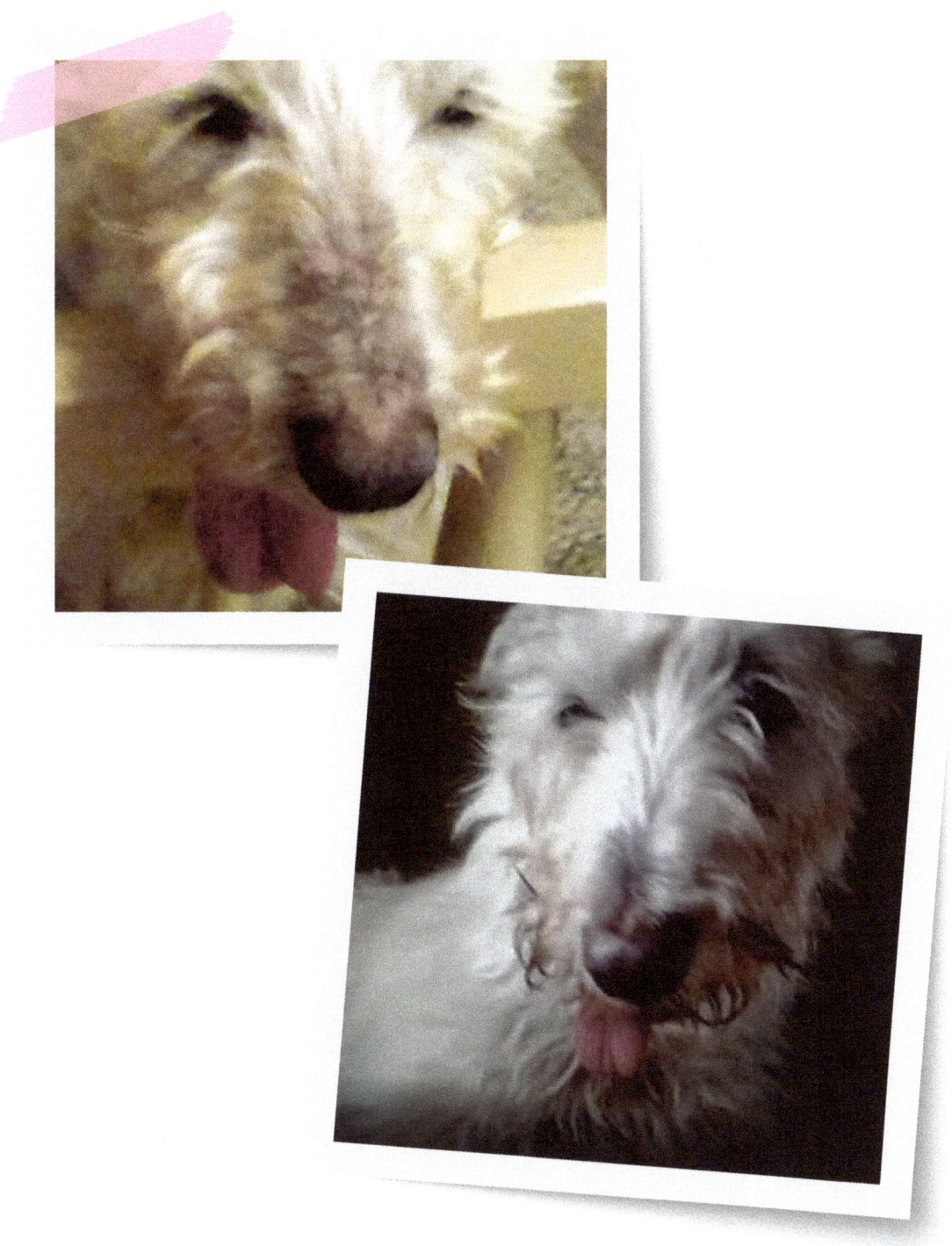

Eyes

What did Sammy see, and how do I look at things?

Sammy's eyes — his essence!

Real love, true love

Sight vs. blindness; often, we can choose to be either!
Super Sammy gained a sparkle of confidence we all need.

Sammy emitted an ethereal glow both *day* and *night*.

Teeth

Spud Teething Ring

For teeth that will never come back, lost through cruelty.

Yet, teething pain remains, as we understand.

Tongue

His tongue was always visible and part of his personality.

Soul's rudder?

Heart's rudder?

Ears

Attentive?

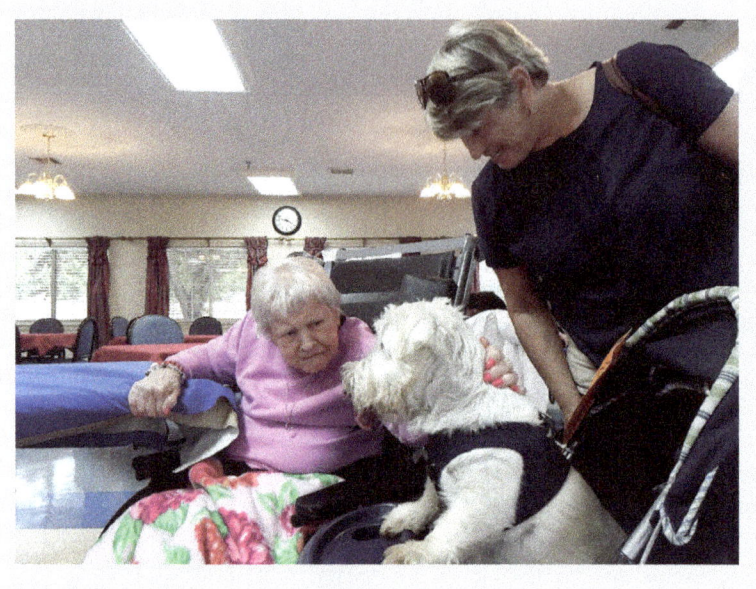

Cannot raise on his own.
Perky with symbols.
Sammy was a natural comfort to any and everyone!

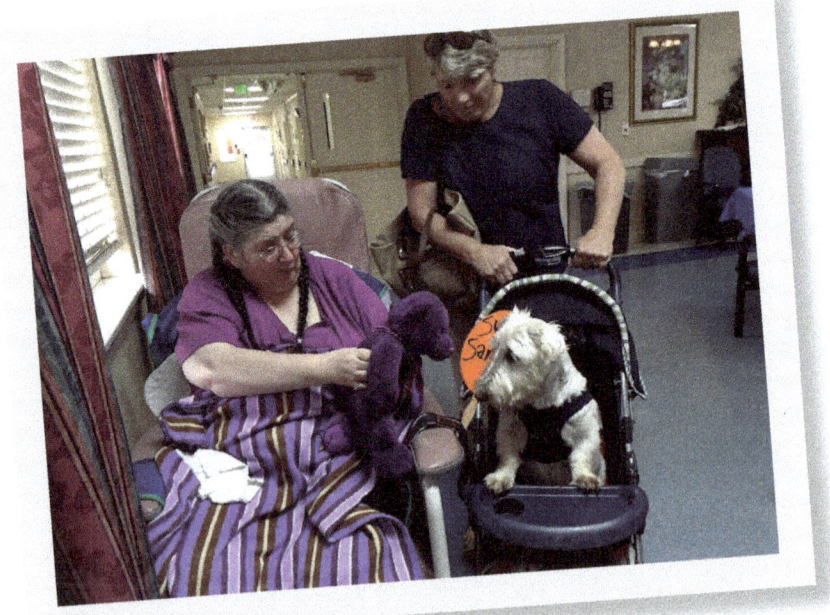

His ears weren't perfect, but his comforting soul was natural.

Much like the heart.

Ears were a follower instead of a guide.

Fur

Coloration

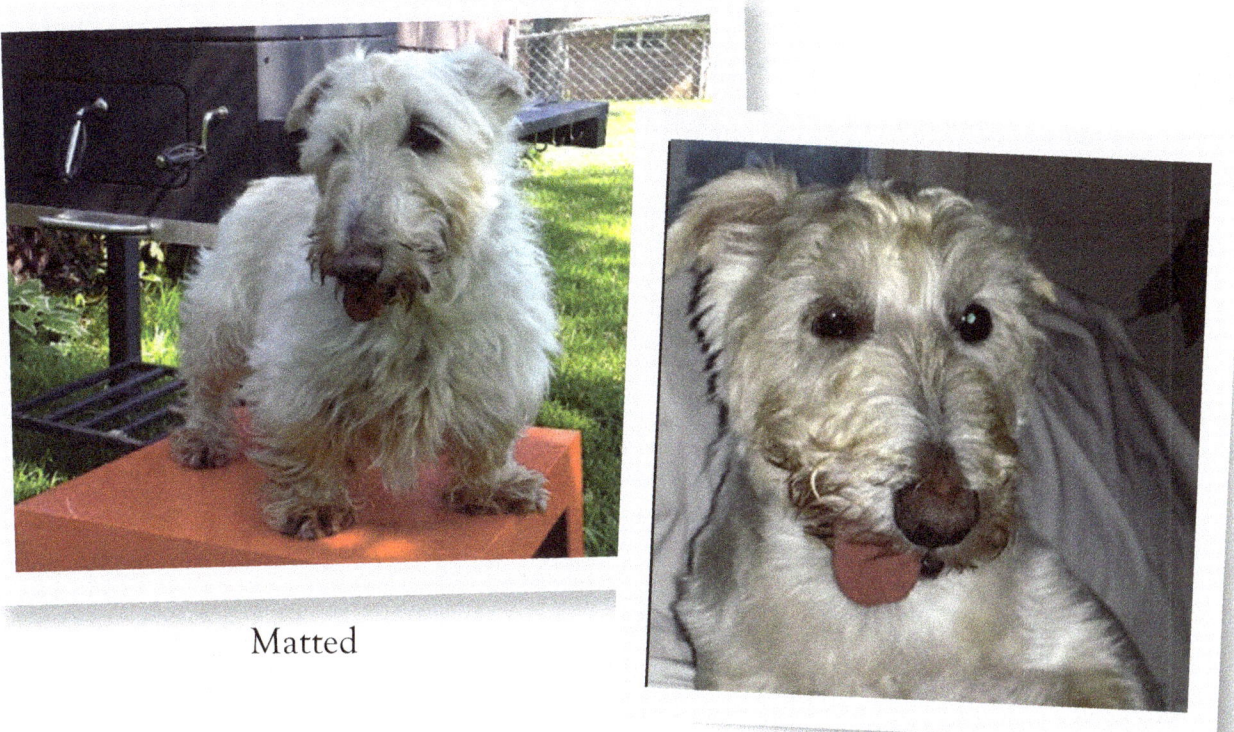

Matted

Ode to An Angel

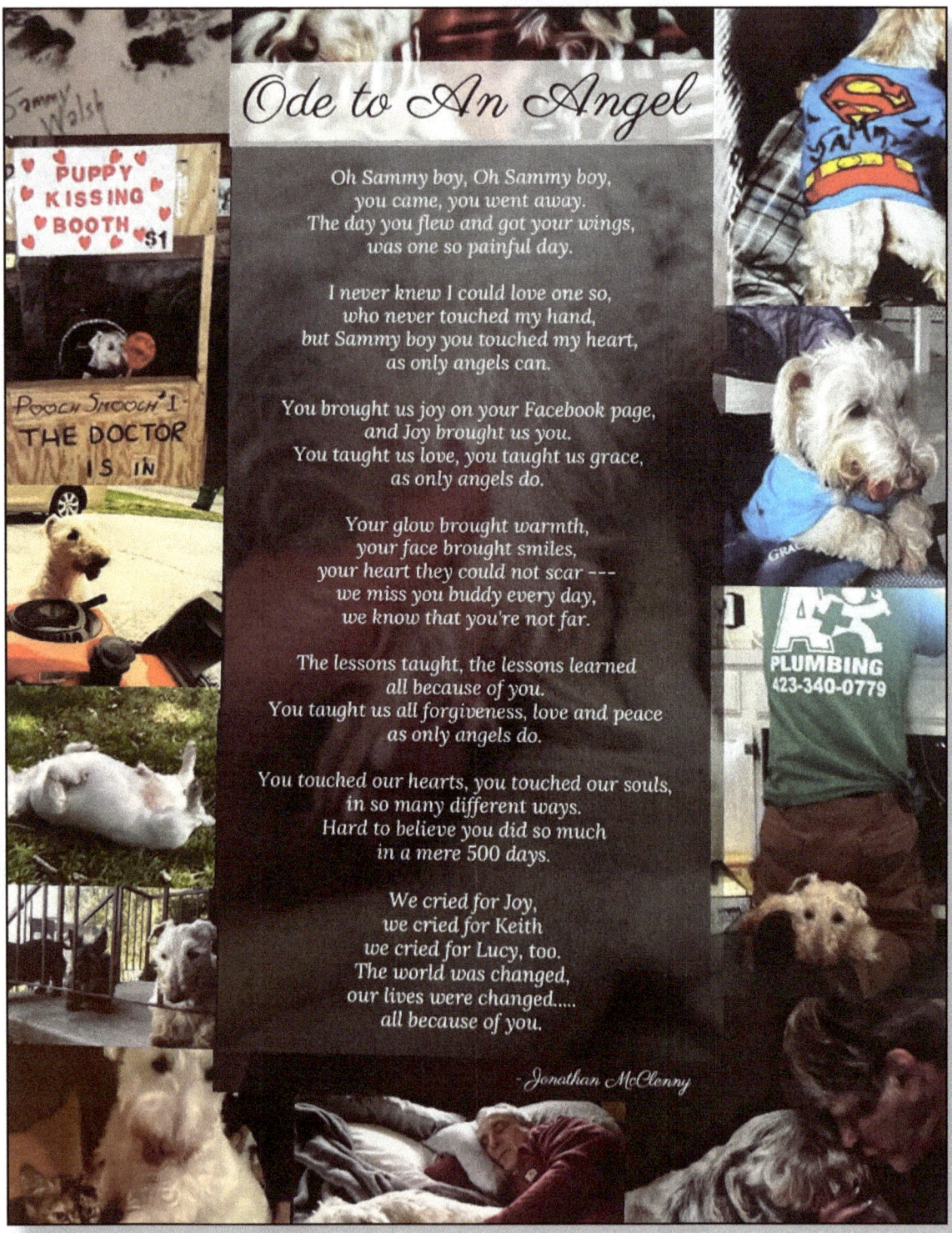

Poem and Print credited to Jonathan McClenny

I Am Ugly

"What We Perceive" vs. "What Is"

"U"
Understanding
Undesirable
Unusual
Unsightly

"G"
Gracious
Grasping
Gentle
Godly

"L"
Lost
Luster
Love
Loathsome

"Y"
Yes, to possibilities! Yesterday is gone! Yesterday's pain, sorrow, and trauma is ugly — just ugly.

Super Sammy

Artwork by Patch Wheatley, UK

Task List

The lawnmower will not start. I'll look it over!

Okay, okay!

Mission

Friendships were made.

Destiny

Desire

Epilogue

I'm a Sammy. Touch someone...now!
"I already know it!" from Joy Walsh.
"I am Sammy."

Online Proclamation

How to rescue dogs?
There are different levels and pieces to the rescue puzzle.
Different parts of the process for different people.
Not everyone is cut out for each facet of the process.
Donations or actual rescue?

www.ingramcontent.com/pod-product-compliance
Lightning Source LLC
Chambersburg PA
CBHW060856090426
42736CB00023B/3491